THE COAST OF BOHEMIA

For Sarah, Jessica, Lachlan and Josephine

Contents

THE COAST OF BOHEMIA

FLEDGLING

lay on its back,
head skewed
into the drowning water,

rain held
in the palm of a flagstone.
The wings

were gestures at themselves,
black, bone-spoked
rags of umbrella;

the taut
sac of belly
was most of it,

yellowish, veined.
No pulse flickered
like a feather beneath a window.

This was no subject
for my poem
about the arts

except that it recalled
the hearing without which
no sparrow falls.

Describe, describe
it seemed to say
like everything

when death
brings the world into focus,
line by line

sharpening flagstone, corpse
and cold rainwater dead
as mercury.

NOTES AND QUERY

They are building a new shopping-mall,
with atrium, in this, the year malls
go out of fashion.

> *The New Age*
> *wears white and carries glass or precious crystals*
> *to tame the cells that are frantic to be diseased.*
> *It also keeps its nose clean.*

When it almost reaches the skylight,
who'll dust the vine?

ANALYSIS

Because the centre of my heart is pure
Confusion, I have not yet brought to light
The shaping trouble that in each of us
Is early set, I'm told. The corridor
    Of dreams has lately given out
On green hills, flowering, commodious

Beyond the brown despondent pastorals
I wrote last year. A woman's in the door,
The sunlight sparking in her hair, her face
Effaced in shadow. Like a cistern that fills
    And flushes, is this nightly chore,
Labouring to a world I cannot place?

If a man hear the high wind promising
There will be happiness, but not for you,
Hear, and pull up the bedclothes like a shell
For fear he may have heard his trouble sing,
    Or tame it to a point of view,
He cannot wish his future very well.

LIBERTY BELL

For some reason,
I wanted to look like Napoleon

or Lafayette –
I forget,

but I stuck my right hand
inside my quilted, lined

and Marshal's anorak
to stare straight back

into my father's camera,
a paramour

of history, the great
man, rising eight.

The picture's lost
or, so to say, gone west.

                        *

Sand, sea, silica, silicon.
I might have lived in California

but, though it seems unlikely,
born here

I was forbidden to be President.
Sand, sea, bikini, daiquiri,

tequila, muscat, grass,
the blur in which I might have missed

the television decades
and, endlessly replayed,

shot through a porthole,
not that you saw the porthole,

the bluey mirled
swirl of the clouds that cloud this world.

SET TEXTS

Cicero, Livy, Caesar
line the walls of a private education.
They absorb chalk and sound
as they once drew history to themselves,
the warm-skinned, unimaginable Clio.

There must be more than one red
maple in Canada, but I remember
only the one, flaming on a hillside of evergreens.
A rough passage. Only I
didn't go sea-sick.

This is a city yearning
to be another city. A flurry of leaves.
The old, shingled hotel vanished
in an icy twinkle
– January, when I hardly went out.

I remember that scarlet
moribund plumage when I think of the white
snail-horns of mustard my daughter moistens
in her halved, painted eggshells.
They feel their way into a covered darkness

as everything must that waits
for the great change, to point up green at heaven,
to fall short, branching
and aimless wishes, empty
accelerations into privacy.

After the States, we drove up
from Southampton to Leeds to sell our house
in a beige Hillman Imp, tame and tiny
after our green gunmetal Rambler.
My veins are a tree planted nowhere.

The outskirts were no longer
the blackened back-to-backs where our daily lived,
where her husband the gardener took each year's
prize for his yard of colour, where their boy, Albert,
had a drum-kit and an apprenticeship.

The new towers had rubble
up to their ankles, kept their measured distance.
Like my placeless public-school accent.
Like the sentences in dead languages it served
through to their period, to their verbs in the perfect tense.

LATE ROMAN

I go out with heavy trudge through cerulean pilasters,
  colonnades overlooking questionable civilisations.
I am not long alone before someone official belabours
  messengers' infuriating dilatoriness extravagantly.

O to let blue paint embody heavens apostate otherwise –
  childhood's overarching unassailable primitiveness!
I? My lot dies after boldly mocking emperors nightfall
  reimagines, forgetfully, triumphantly, conquistadors.

GOING AWAY TO SCHOOL AT THIRTEEN

We parked on the Embankment, which,
I remembered, meant near the Tate.
During our sandwiches, my father warned me
against too close friendships with older boys.
Almost his words.

Closing my sponge-bag,
I was jeering at Harold Wilson's latest
when a monitor, picking up
on my interests, invited me to tea
tomorrow.

I chewed a bun,
transfixed
by his paintbrushes in a jar
half-full of a cloudy liquid that must be sperm.

DIALLING TONE

I was listening through the night
for your breaths in another city.

Dawn's a brisk business,
putting a bruised black-yellow finish

on gaunt clouds; outside, a foxglove
hides in itself to sleep the rain off.

THE NATURE POEM

Walking the fields at dawn
you hear the birdcry
start, a punch of sound, while grey light
irradiates the false front of a house
older than it pretends.

And that is all. There is no time
to think of your imagination,
how it enspheres the whole
into the sheer experience you have
years afterwards, no time at all.

What you remember isn't birds,
or light, or sullen stucco.
It is the sudden coming to,
the knowing you were lost,
a moment, to yourself, so what you were

rose like that gathered sound
and stood away from you.
Aimless, homeless,
you grasped your life
would not be in your keeping.

LANGUEDOC

Red earth like open hands,
a shrug of mountains

and a volcanic greengage
burst by its own strength.

The green field
reaches a yellow field

and peters out.
A child

on flushed legs
runs to the edge

and runs back.
Small blue butterflies sew the camera.

That the veil of the world parts
is also an illusion.

GLANCES OFF
in memory of my father

Afterwards, in the pub, I asked if Mailer
had been right when he called him irresistible
to women. *Oh yes, yes,* she breathed,
gazing into the optics, lost. That

was the night Robert Lowell stole my girl's heart,
the night I like to think he stole it.
I had taken her to his reading, secretly
to show off that I sort of knew him.

What he said comes back.
He'd met you twice. *I remember
your father. He's a very
gentle man.* In his rubbed voice.

Prophetic epitaph!
Daddy, I am still standing on my first bed.
Your warm hands pull down
my white teeshirt with the small blue elephants on.

CLASS

Or that man, now a doctor,
who'd rather
ostentatiously brought his new boyfriend.

The poets
to be read were prescribed for us
by the setters of crosswords.

Who could see,
wind flailing at the empty stable,
what we should be?

There was a time when people smoked in bed
alone. They lay back and watched the ceiling
repeating headlights from the lonesome road.

It was the country place
of a financial journalist
let to a friend.

When we piled back inside, that poor boy and girl
who left the bus angrily before our stop
had just arrived

and were quite unfazed by the Nordic sailor.

ONE DOWN

Here is an eye
on the bow of a barge –
piratical, a shark's,

slick as a cheese-wire,
it cuts downstream
like instinct

honed, like a gymnast
practicing through the air
her double somersault.

Her trainer's hands
nipped and tucked
like moulding

ice as it thawed,
too fast to see,
patting or petting

his dream of flight.
The barge thrums
to the beat of its engine,

dead, dull,
reliable.
I went on one,

a prep-school holiday;
we'd moored in Rugby'
the night I fell,

taking a hanging
loose sheaf of grass
for dry land,

so the boy in the galley
ran up the steps
to see a monster,

dripping, beweeded,
dark
against the darkness.

Emma, your death,
falling off Lundy,
was much like that.

Puffin-shit sprang
to my mind when I heard,
the night I wept

in a tight
blue room,
you smeared with it,

washed up,
anonymous.
I hover still

over the riddle
whether you meant it,
like a trainer

nipping and tucking, wanting
something
exactly judged

from your meaningless plunge.
Twin pairs of shoes
in my friend's

country bedroom
figured you ice
thawing

then you set,
gone, gone
as an old fashion.

The barge thrums –
you'd smile at this –
like Charon's ferry,

but for the absence
of other shores,
its dead eye set

on the grey wash and throb
you have been rinsed by,
the open sea

you embraced,
I must expect,
not to arise from, dripping.

STANZAS

Here are the shells our daughter
brought me on Brighton beach,
too small for ears, for even junk
jewellery ear-rings, white fans

with delicate brown fringes
that cannot hear the sea.
An ammonite chipped out by luck,
the background radiation

from the first nanoseconds
the stones remember, echo.
There was the bombed hotel
restored, the rougher, mugging

tyre-slashing district
with sotto voce pubs,
the dolphinarium
and all its pent

intelligence.
They walked on water.
They poured their bulk through hoops.
They beat time with their tails.

Hurtling accurate gentle tons
they'd leap, nip a fish like a kiss
from the girl trainer's mouth.
Listening to the focussed shells

of headphones, fortune-hunting nostalgia
kept me up half the night
in our friend's flat. I watch the sea's
turbulent peristalsis,

shingle dragged up and down
the face of each new wave.
Echo-locating dolphins
pass beyond rank or gender

into telepathy, it's said,
so that each I
has fluid edges, feels
each individual hurt.

Fists in the pockets of her buttoned,
mannish coat, loneliness drifts
outside the palmist's curtained booth.
We harden with desire.

Tonight on the polished bar,
the glug of optics:
I thought of ranged
bare platforms,

mailbags, early editions,
rain shaken
out of the night sky over Crewe.
Two in the morning,

your head sleeps in my lap,
dreams an island where trees
huddle in clefts, bare upland pools
lie staring at the naked sky.

THE DREAM OF GALLIFREY

Tamarisk feathers,
high sunset cloud,
sunset the usual
eight minutes late.
The next star
is more than four years back.

Our eyes adjust.
Space crawls with stars and curves
to cup them like the red
plastic solitaire board
my brothers knelt at.
Their light drags, red.

Everything falls away
from our horizon,
backward and out,
only machines
hear the dim heat,
the howl

of the beginning
everything flies from
like shaky deer
out of a flaming forest,
the moment vacuum
wobbled and burst.

The pretty constellations
are strung out
like a perspective exercise
and move as we move,
too slowly
to change our quick behaviour.

When my parents
installed their first fridge,
did they reckon
they were wrecking the planet?
Well, we blame them
as surely as the stars,

unwilling to concede
time points to us to find for what
wedding, what funeral,
earth trails the heavens like a veil.
I was a boy
when men walked

on the face of the huntress.
Gently bending incoming light
she rises, less
than a minute behind us,
earth's ashen, ruined sister
no doctor heals.

TWO VERTICALS, FOUR SEMICIRCLES

Virtual koala,
notional tree –
how can we see what isn't there?

The abstract nouns accumulate like clouds
while, round the back,
there is a munch of eucalyptus.

*

Riddle of seeing,
that it will come as a woman

approaches, or a man
approaches, love,

whispering the beloved name,
holding it out for you like a dish of fruit.

*

I have seen thought thought
into a skein of pulsing light,

a desk toy's
tremolo solitude,

a gizmo
playing the stars. It sings like ice.

*

A wrist snakes.
Bruised eyes. A rapid sketch
of loyalty and beating.

Appearing is the wonder,
before the story, the mere breath
of *Apples with a Raindrop* in their still life.

ALETHEIA

Landscape is lonely
whatever man
most elsewhere; here, wind sings
the pylon-stridden valley,
a cup of hills.

The city nests
like rancour,
the city nestles in.
Wind romps
in the limbs of the spindly trees

across the river, raindrops
frill and fly
from black twigs,
the unconcealed
shines on the face of earth

that lifts to rain
like tilting to be kissed
though not,
a gust of joy
off desolation.

BELIEF

My father raised his hands once,
making a moving wall.
The bat in the conservatory
vanished no less politely.

OCTETS
around Mandelstam

People feel the city come to a point,
the whole boiling sweat and tremble.
Who knows? Perhaps the wind leaves barracks
with fixed rain to probe ditch and alley.

Waiting-room dread. To leave this patient life
the poor gather nettles on waste ground.
I have had the last of our bitter coffee.
You gave it me and did not tell me.

*

The hills ran together to greet me
then ran apart, opening to the sea
and the white resort on its yellow horseshoe,
the steep valley a wrinkle on an almond.

I was a sparrow in the carriage,
looking and looking, threadbare, chirruping.
Our burly-shouldered engine rocked and swayed
like a bully's generous, spendthrift day.

*

Slippery granite and the mica night:
I must be ground between them, heart
like a servant somebody had to let go.
Packed trams, jars with the boys, jokes about

rape: when it feels the world fall short
of itself, the heart goes on like a footloose
pebble in the open mouth of a great ravine.
Its death-cry, just a plink, is still a cry.

HOME AND AWAY

Oxford. It is one of those tentative spring days
I keep crossing over to sunlit pavements
from chilly shadow, here to use the libraries
and to read single-mindedly until my reading
tames my heart to the rhythm of the turning pages.

The shops and cinemas have different names.
I don't know how many changes of set I've missed
in the seductive, heartless city.
All I recognise is the strangers
like the failures in a repertory company,

in character forever, while the changing young
are soon supplanted by their understudies.
It's odd, thinking that if these are 'old haunts'
the ghosts are younger than myself. The house
you lived in when I met you, it's been gentrified

much, I suppose, as we've more money now.
It has kept pace with and forgotten us,
our friends, the life we had, finally,
to leave to make a living. Home is another city
where I know more people by sight than I can talk to

so we box the compass for friends and family
– as though south meant anything in our circle, tiny
as a preserved steam railway. There sleepless still, I
   browsed for coma.
Goethe, cyclothymic, took off for Italy
where the earth holds its composition and you play

your metres on your lover's body. Love
I cried on the hard healthy mattress and a kiss
was placed exactly on the corner of my mouth,
an understanding in the dark I couldn't grasp, waking
painfully late, if better read in pharmacology.

I am so tired I can hardly unfold the map.
A motorway on stilts puts the dimly
familiar road that reels us out of London in the shade,
then it swings away from us with disdain
and the wire fences I remember just aren't here.

The wooden cafés slump with resignation, flapping
their faded ice-cream signs like women weeping dusting,
the low vegetation is what it always was,
stunted trees, grey grass, knots of tenacious gorse,
hidden brilliant weeds neglect and law protect.

London thinned out to humbler terraces, then vanished
    with the last
three fabrics, roofs bare timbers now, not worth
    developing
in the sandscape between valley and rising, richer hills.
My heart no longer rises with their rising
or their dormitory affluence, the steakhouses,

the reconditioned pubs with real ale for weekends and us,
these villages I passed at the start of each school term.
    Dreams have moved
to smaller houses, Arcadian stencils done by hand, green
    flowers, long
blue leaves quickening the white of a bathroom door,
airbrushed blue dancers melting on the blue-grey kitchen
    floor.

SCENT

Flittering hummingbird, here-and-gone presences
that may be skin-deep (for you, no depth at all),
what are they? Evanescent as the scent that lingers
on jerseys of the men who love you and embrace you
vanishing in the laundromat. You showed me photos.

You were a child. These things were not yet thinkable.
Yet, so younger, so insignificantly younger, you can tell
    me
fuck off with all the hurt helplessness can feel.
You must have been a little older than the palms,
fully grown with tiny sharp dandelion heads.

The West Riding, Tunisia, the childhoods
we didn't share, spin like a dream: I would wake gripped
in your tight arms flushed with the night's warmth – to be
    thought
circumspectly, as though you heard. Can what the
    unpromised
body promises be, in conscience, dreamed of?

Like dandelion fluff, years flew off calendars
to thicken albums, choices in work, love, travel,
life changing to a way of life. Skimming the pages
you approached, and were more apart from, what you
    are,
the pictures feeling falser the more they tried to catch
    you.

You are more chary than a flickering butterfly,
than a moth of the lime on branches lit by lanterns:
I only say what everybody says, or so you say,
I, an echo in the wind-tunnel of desire it's perilous
for one so streamlined, yet so skittering, to chance.

FROM THE COAST OF BOHEMIA

Battered raffia, Russian vines are dangling
like an abandoned therapy, for my doctor's garden's
Rousseauesque foliage is late this spring.
The only hope for it is time's cure-all
and I reach the end of another consultation. Home:

children have drawn with charcoal on the stones.
I am not incurably sad
although I have forgotten all my games
and remember only a silver Colt I lost in my sandpit
and found rusted, the trigger-action gone.

Somehow the one my grandfather sent
by chance for my next birthday never felt the same.
It is like my friend's Czech friend insisting
I spit upon your Shakespeare
with his filthy geography.

Do you suppose we could have been restrained
if we had had that legendary coastline?
You couldn't call a Colt the equaliser now.
The stick-men stare blindly, eyes bigger than their heads.
The bedraggled, tangled garden is bowed with longing.

THE CHILD WHO WENT AWAY

Look, the exile on Main Street tips his stetson forward to
    screen
vertical sun. The sheriff greets him. He has become his
    name.
He is involved with neither man nor woman yet respected
for his adroitness on a horse, the righteous way he
    handles
the old man's helicopter, only chaffs the lovely daughter.
I slept through the hurricane. The city shook in its river,
waters that cross and cross their current like eyes looking
    for eyes
across a room. The morning after, trees like whales,
    flanks to slap.
Hands shushed the broken grain. Some wept. It might be
    a heath we passed
one Christmas: bushy feathered grass made all such waste
    places one,

for in one I lost my red Red Indian rubber dagger,
My pipe-dream, day-dream hero and the hookers pass
    time. One day
the woman will arrive by air, connecting from the red-eye
through Houston, Dallas or Fort Worth. Bad health,
    poverty, terror
make for faith, but more so this ache for the heavenly
    country.
We knew a man who lived under a pseudonym, his own
    name.
Only a handful of guests at his parties knew the other.
Once, he kissed me goodnight, in another county, the
    famous
writer who hid his new book in two fawn manilla folders.
To tell secrets and keep yourself a secret. What pasts
    doorstep

the vagrant heart, send it inside to fray a paper napkin.
I saw more than was meant in the incorrigible eyes, the
observations that must be passed, or hoped I did, in a
    brusque
memo or two friends walking off in conversation. The
    clouds
burst with their own weight, bars of water holding me in
    like ribs
caging the sucking, squirting heart. The squirming heart.
    Whatever
this is, it is not expunged by rain rod or rain whip hissing
on tiles like canvas. Love yes word known to all men
    seldom heard
for eyes for lips given given back for lips for eyes tender
word rarely heard. The rain stops. The sky pulls itself
    together.

Dry gaunt wind combs the earth with a sharpened
    pointlessness like loss.
Makes my day. As my child put it, playing, roaring his
    car back
across the table, *The sea's closed today*. Elsewhere, its fist
    slammed
into secluded cliffs. If I lived in this flattened country
I would want the resources for it. It is not the expanse
but the choking narrowness of its August when the rich
    leaves
make a brilliant conversation, passing their topic, light,
round with an end-of-period fertility of ideas
at angles, gilded summer, terrifies me. It absorbs me,
its veridian suction, its almost satisfying gulp.

Unfurled, syntactic, written to a family prescription,
fingering down into the grit and muck of winter yet up
into the humourless woolly chaos of clouded mornings,
the stripped tree in the eye of the view, which gathers the
    wide fields
to lay them back out with its own place-holding solidity,
says nothing to our condition, seeing that the one time it
has to bear rises through its green invisible skin-deep
    veins
and collaborates with drought and shade to find it its
    unique
shape in the air, yet, to be read without system, browsed
    on spec,
is what it offers always, being both open and opaque.

HOSPITAL

Where the hedge had been broken
I ducked through, smashing
nettle and fern, angling back
out of sight of the drive, down
to the edge of a lake
tucked in under a wooded hillside.

There was an island with one bare tree,
ivy and knitting grasses, ordinary
enough to make
silence of the mind
a moment. Amnesia
is amnesty. Why was I here?

Somebody else was cruel,
drunken, unsteady, wobbled off
to the secluded clinic,
chocked windows, plastic mirror.
Take these,
they will dissolve the tremor.

A suitcase full of books.
What was my daily paper?
Outside, beyond the trees,
at one edge of the field
the stone cattle-trough
was a cryptic sarcophagus.

Desertion is betrayal: I imagined
the winter lawn, unshaven, haggard,
the sandpit waterlogged
as though with tears, the shears
I never oiled, the whole
uneasy garden

where the lost children tottered, wind
smacked the strained washing
and petals burrowed
into the lawn, heads down, shaken
like a shrew I once saved
in a flowerbed from a cat;

it raised all its tiny
courage and bit me,
shivering on my palm.
I had taken the lives
of my family in my palm,
taken myself seriously

away.
That day, the little island stayed
my headlong longing to be ill
and irresponsible,
bareness answering mine
as greater bareness would

in a dreamed desolate flat
above the city.
If and then, if and then:
logical prophecies,
distracted heart.
It was time to be going back.

MANIA

It is easy to write yourself off
in your own eyes, easier than at first
the eyes of others, though you do it
finally with some gross manoeuvre

like a motorbike's diagonal skid
smearing the parapets of ruts
on a track overhung with nettles
that ushers, utters you towards the towpath

where the primitive washed light of your former
walks is a punitive reminder
of the little trapped fragments of the sky
that joyrider slewed through and flung

gobsmacked into the heavens' lap then down
on this brown gravelled featureless trudge
you go on with your reddening hands
bloating your already distended pockets

feeling the cigarettes unpaid bills
tickets that claim you as a citizen,
that name you, calling you to fatal
decencies and the order of the day

for when everything you have done resounds
dishonour there is still this grind back
to the red houses, here, between the river
and the obsolete millstream's shiny face

where you found the loneliness you were
perversely seeking as the city
closed its ears and you felt your pleas thrown
back at you with a venomous reproach

so keep your dreams of what is past love,
the invisible one for whom desire leaps
beyond the limits of your chained blood
that, as you plod like a horse's dutiful ghost,

when a duck jumps and scatters water
you feel something out of it all
condemns whatever happens
to be your life and you go wondering,

you exist, you do not exist, damp gusts
peel the earth gently bare, look, the mist
throws back a limb that turns
into a gesture, then a wish, then nothing.

DORA MARKUS
from Montale

I

It was where the wooden jetty
sticks out at Porto Corsini over the deep sea
and scattered men, almost stationary, plunge
or hoist nets. With a hand's
gesture you indicated the invisible
other shore, your homeland.
Then we followed the canal as far as the city's
little harbour, shiny with grime,
in the lowland where a sluggish springtime
sank without memory.

And here where an obsolete life
is speckled with a gentle
Oriental anxiety
your words were iridescent, like the scales
of the gasping mullet.

Your restlessness makes me think
of the migrant birds that hit lighthouses
on stormy evenings:
your gentleness too is a storm,
it eddies without seeming to,
and its lulls are rarer still.
I don't know how, exhausted, you hold out
in that pool
of indifference which is your heart; maybe
an amulet preserves you, one you keep
next to your lipstick,
powder-puff, nail-file; a white mouse,
an ivory one; and that's how you exist!

II
By now, in your Carinthia
with its myrtles in bloom, and its ponds,
leaning over the bank you are watching
the timid carp that yawns
or you trace, over the limetrees, across the bristling
spires, the ignition sparks
of evening and in the water a blaze
of awnings from quays and boarding-houses.

That evening which spreads out
over the humid basin carries nothing
with the heartbeat of engines
but cries of geese and a decor
of snow-white porcelain tells
the blackened mirror which sees you
changed a tale of untroubled
blunders and engraves it
where the sponge cannot reach.

Your legend, Dora!
But it is written already in those looks
from men with proud,
weak side-whiskers in majestic gold
portraits and it returns
in every chord squeezed
from the wheezing harmonica while day
is dimming, always later on.

It is written there. The evergreen
laurel persists
for cooking, the unsilenced voice,
Ravenna is distant, a fierce
faith distils venom.
What does it ask of you? Nobody yields
voice, legend or destiny . . .
But it's late, always later on.

MEMO

Poems remember
what I cannot forget.

There are moments of wanting to be well
entirely. Yesterday –
was it? –
I saw the lightning stand straight up

between buildings
like a young woman's flashing body
white at her first unrobing,
or like a scar that healed forever.

The trolley hushes
the corridor
like a chaplain in suede shoes.
Frivolous noise

that might be silence
or her face drinking mine.
The abrupt rush
of my hands to a clench like prayer.

THE SINGLE LIFE

The aquarium in the Chinese take-away
bumps the noses of gross, bulb-headed fish whose eyes
    plead
for the excellence of their trapped souls like postulant
anorexics floundering in fatness. They mouth
and mouth but cannot reproduce the costive
knowing vowels of girls at tables in the restaurant
with their assured, imperious 'You eat that this way',
nuzzling the bottom for missed feed, expertly spitting
    gravel.

I wait over a glass of white wine. Through plastic strips
masking a door, smells drift and a television
shows me some muddy water and a dead tree
trying to drown. The rains have come and gone
like a net curtain when the breeze turns.
Lions assemble at the water, giving
each other the odd sideways high-table glance.
A snake swallows a frog. The legs stop moving.

BY THE FIRESIDE

The cat stares into the fire
like a god with imperfect prescience.

All the Norse gods could know
was that their world was doomed.
Baldur died by a dart of mistletoe.

– Ah yes, we kissed
once, in the quarter-light before dawn
when nothing seemed impossible. Such transience

and such desire.
It was a clear night; for once, no mist,
simply the hard-edged moon

whose inattentive gaze
plays
again over the rough yard where I dreamed we dreamed.

ASTRONOMY

Tonight, walking home,
I heard drought
gasp. The dust between paving-stones.

I thought of that other summer
I missed,
studying for exams,

your stories of a pond
just vanishing,
the stranded, staring fish.

They may not be lovers whom I saw
but their eyes met and slid apart
like fencing with knitting-needles.

When she went off, his eyes
ran down to glance
off her hip into peopled space.

It was late afternoon across the city.
Bright unrebuffed
sun in the open air.

Children's high open voices.
It seems, their tears so quickly turn
to laughter,

feelings
blow through us on their way
from star to star.

CLIENTS

It was mellowed before it met the sun,
this very modern, neo-classical
arched facade where the health-food shop,
a sports shop and a jeweller's glittering
velvet-bedded titanium and copper
are neighbours. Signs for loans, shoes, journeys;
girls in short skirts to furnish them. Eight years
and the place has changed faster than I notice,
red brick junked for the honey-coloured new.

*

McTaggart supposed time did not exist,
that we stood, ignorant, in eternity
already, seen through by each other's love.
He would have wised up seeing time as money.
It can be bought or borrowed or advanced,
stolen or snatched or wasted. Time is lost
in a swirl of anxiety and jasmine
until at the last reckoning we plead
for credit in a windowless basement room.

*

We have our dreams of reconciliation;
yes, and our fantasies of sudden rain
whipping us naked on the blackened street.
Then we should know what need is, and what love.

NEW YEAR'S DAY

It looked more like an excavation than a building-site:
trailing grass, mud, a sense of fields gone but not yet
   replaced,
of absence, expectation, hope. Our parents led us on,
three of us in red balaclavas and what kind of coat
I don't remember. I would think we could fly a kite here

like the true bamboo and brown paper one I'd had in Leeds
and flown on a waste patch, clover, like an enclave of moor
not far above our house; I thought and fought on through
   the wind
round an angle of hillside to a view of concrete stumps
that ended the first phase of the library-cum-bookshop.

Physics was on an upper level. We went through swing
   doors.
If a glazed walkway entered another building, the floors
missed by a jagged inch I tripped on. This was the future,
my father's future, mine. It smelt of air-conditioning
and green linoleum. It was a place where people worked.

There were geese on the artificial third lake already,
droppings like crumbling fir-cones, in the landscape
   Constable
also adjusted, a tree here or there, round the focal
red house that was now a refectory and conference-suite.
I had seen the painting in a Washington gallery,

stretched up, crewcut, almost to touch it, asked in the
   odd twang
it would take prep-school to kick out of me whether the
   park
was as it was. It wasn't. A stilled bulldozer's share loomed
cold to touch by the stones like stepping-stones that
   trotted down
through swirls of mud and grass to the water in case of fire.

Cloud thickens, darker than the dull cathedral leads I see
at all street-ends, omening rain. The day flickers and
   streams.
Out of my children's bedroom window, I glimpse them at
   play
in the garden that will change to a childhood memory.
Love, they have carved a passage out where you cut the
   brush back

under that blowsy tree, the big-bosomed, billowing one
that has shed its leaves and is wiry like poorly permed
   hair.
Winter-smashed flowerbeds loll and sway as the wind
   eddies
restlessly, listlessly, inattentively ruffling heads
so that last summer's gold, almost gone, tugs its
   shadowed roots.

They are like trees and they are not like trees. The trees
   go on
without us, any of us, not like children who outlive
but at a longer pace, settling back to what was before.
Names peel from signposts and the lost blue plastic sack
   is crushed
by nettles in the slow exhalation of a landscape.

When I laid my father in the wet oblivious earth
an inundating wind had drowned the priest's words and
   the strip
of webbing was stiff in my stiff fingers. It's New Year's
   Day
and I hover behind the window irresolutely
wishing the reeds might prick up round our winter-
   freshened pond.